PUFFIN BOOKS
AMMA, TAKE ME TO SHIRDI

Bhakti Mathur took to writing in 2010 when she created the popular Amma, Tell Me series of children's picture books about Indian festivals and mythology. After a long stint as a banker, she now juggles her time between her writing, her passion for yoga and long-distance running, and her family. She lives in Hong Kong with her husband, their two children and two dogs. She holds a master of fine arts degree in creative writing from the University of Hong Kong, is a freelance journalist and contributes regularly to the South China Morning Post. When not writing or running after her young boys, Bhakti is happiest curled up with a book in one hand and a hot cup of chai in the other. To know more, visit her at www.bhaktimathur.com.

Priyankar Gupta is an animation film designer and visual storyteller. He is associated with various publishing houses as an illustrator for children's books and also works as a pre-visualizer for TV commercials and feature films. He is a visiting faculty member and mentor in various design institutes across the country.

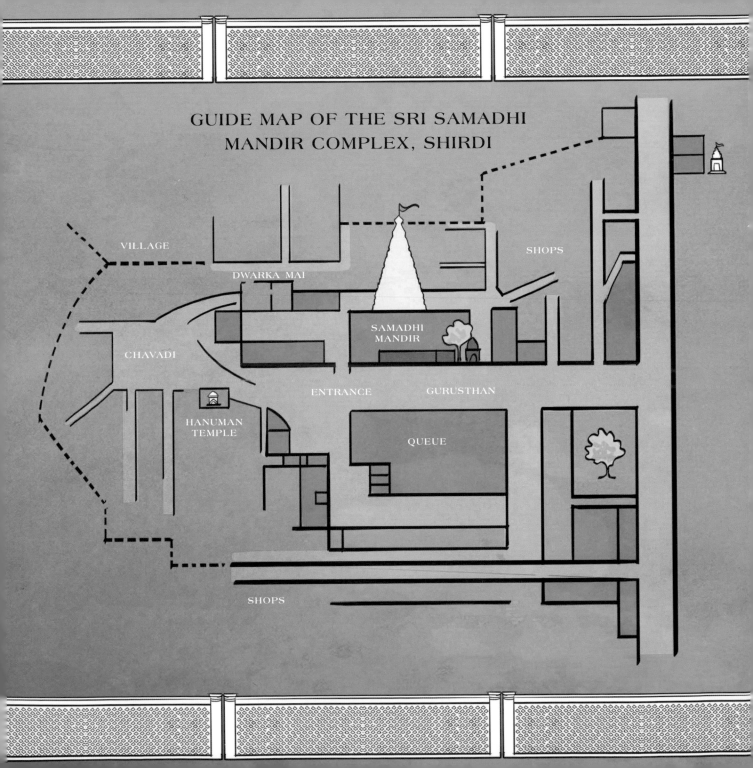

Amma, Take Me to
Shirdi

BHAKTI MATHUR

Illustrations by Priyankar Gupta

PUFFIN BOOKS

An imprint of Penguin Random House

PUFFIN BOOKS

USA | Canada | UK | Ireland | Australia
New Zealand | India | South Africa | China

Puffin Books is part of the Penguin Random House group of companies
whose addresses can be found at global.penguinrandomhouse.com

Published by Penguin Random House India Pvt. Ltd
4th Floor, Capital Tower 1, MG Road,
Gurugram 122 002, Haryana, India

First published in Puffin Books by Penguin Random House India 2019

Text copyright © Bhakti Mathur 2019
Series copyright © Penguin Random House India 2019
Illustrations copyright © Priyankar Gupta 2019

ISBN 9780143448174

Typeset in Agmena Pro
Printed at Aarvee Promotions, India

www.penguin.co.in

For
Anurag, Shiv and Veer

CONTENTS

AUTHOR'S NOTE

The Amma, Take Me series is an attempt to introduce children to the major Indian religions and faiths through their important places of worship. Styled as the travelogues of a mother and her two young children, these books link history, tradition and mythology to bring alive the major temples, churches, mosques and mausoleums of India in an engaging and non-preachy way.

The stories emphasize universal values and the message of love and tolerance central to all faiths. I hope that this journey of Amma and her children will inspire you to embark on your own travels with your children, and I hope that you will enjoy reading these books as much as I enjoyed writing them.

Lastly, these works are a reflection of my personal interpretation of the faith and traditions that these timeless monuments represent. I am far from being an authority on religion or on Indian religious history, and while I have made every effort to ensure that the factual and historical information in these books is correct, I do not assume and hereby disclaim any liability to any party for any loss, damage or disruption caused by errors or omissions.

'How many runs do we need to win?' asked Veer leaning forward.

'20 off 15 balls,' answered Shiv biting his nails.

'C'mon India!' cried out Veer, his fists clenched tightly in his nervousness.

'That's a four! Dhoni's hit a four,' screamed Shiv, and both the boys jumped in their seats in excitement.

'Cricket, cricket, cricket!' muttered Amma under her breath.

The three were travelling in a car, with the two boys huddled over an iPad, while Amma looked out the window. They were on their way to the small town of Shirdi, a few hours' drive from Mumbai, to visit the shrine of Sai Baba, one of the most revered and loved saints of India.

'Can you two stop staring at the screen and look up for a few minutes,' scolded Amma. But the boys remained oblivious, not only to her glares but also to the scenery outside. The drive from Mumbai to Shirdi was taking them up and through the picturesque northern half of the Western Ghats, the series of mountain ranges that run all along the western coast of the Indian peninsula. Lush rolling hills spread out in front and all around them like a huge cloak, covered with patches of green, yellow and brown. From a few carved rocky outcrops in the distance, waterfalls hung like silvery threads reaching down to the valleys below. The countryside was dotted with small villages and settlements, and herds of cows and sheep grazed lazily along the fields next to the highway.

After further needling, Shiv deigned to reply.

'Wait Amma, it's the last over,' he said, staring intently at the screen.

'And there's the winning run!' shouted Veer a few minutes later, raising his arms in the air in victory.

'Amma, we beat New Zealand by seven wickets, and Dhoni scored fifty runs!' said Shiv.

'The lord be praised!' said Amma, rolling her eyes. 'Now can you look out and see what you have been missing.'

Their car had now started climbing up a winding uphill section of the highway.

'Veer, look!' said Shiv, pointing to ivory-coloured windmills that lined the tops of some hills in the distance.

'Wow! The hands of the windmill look like the hands of a giant clock!' said Veer.

The three spent the next ten minutes taking in the scenes around them till Veer turned to Amma and asked, 'When are we going to reach Shirdi?'

'In an hour or so,' said Amma.

'What are we going to do till then?' groaned Shiv. 'The match is over.'

'Maybe, we can watch a movie!' said Veer, looking up at Amma hopefully.

'No more screen time,' said Amma firmly as she took the iPad and put it in her bag.

'But Amma . . .' complained Shiv.

'Shiv, look at that!' said Veer, interrupting him. He was pointing to a large procession of people walking ahead in the distance, along the side of the road. Shiv rolled down the car window and they could hear the rhythmic beats of the *dhol* as their car drew nearer. The excitement and fervour among the group was palpable.

A few were playing the drums with great gusto, some were chanting 'Om Sai Namo Nama, Jai Jai Sai Namo Nama' while others were clapping enthusiastically. In the middle of the procession, a team of four men was walking with a golden palanquin, supported on their shoulders. The palanquin was draped with strings of marigolds on all four sides.

'Amma, what are they carrying?' asked Veer, straining his neck to take a closer look as they drove past the palanquin. In the center of the platform was a large white marble statue of a man seated on a pedestal. The figure was bedecked with a bright green robe embroidered with gold motifs. A matching green cloth was tied across the forehead. A garland of marigold flowers rested around the idol's neck.

'They are devotees of Sai Baba and are carrying his idol,' answered Amma.

'Did Sai Baba look like that?' asked Shiv. 'I like his bandana!'

'Yes and no,' said Amma. 'His face looks so real, just like him. But he never wore the soft silk clothes that he is dressed in here. He wore a simple white robe, which was torn and stitched up in so many places that it looked more like patchwork. He begged for food every day, making his rounds with a begging bowl. His home was a dilapidated mosque where he spent most of his adult life. It still stands in Shirdi today,' said Amma.

'Can we go see it?' asked Veer, eagerly.

'Yes,' said Amma. 'That is why we are going to Shirdi. To pay our respects at Baba's tomb in the Sri Samadhi Temple and to see where and how Sai Baba lived. You can also see the clothes he wore and a few of his other belongings.'

'The same clothes that he wore when he was alive?' asked Veer with a gasp.

'Yes, the same clothes, Veer. They are kept in a small museum for people to look at,' said Amma.

'Baba is buried in a temple?' asked Shiv looking confused. 'I thought you said he lived in a mosque.'

'That's a good question, Shiv,' said Amma. 'To understand why, you will have to hear the story of Baba's life first.'

'Tell me, tell me,' said Shiv.

Before Amma could answer, Veer interrupted saying, 'Where are these people going, Amma?'

'To Shirdi,' replied Amma.

'What!' said Shiv in disbelief. 'Are they walking all the way? That's so far!'

'Yes, it is,' said Amma nodding her head. 'Shirdi is almost 240 km from Mumbai. That is like walking six marathons! People walk for seven to eight hours every day and rest at night in guest houses along the way. It takes a week to reach Shirdi. Not only that, people walk to Shirdi from all parts of India and it often takes much longer than a week.'

'Wow!' said Shiv, flabbergasted.

'Amma, look! So many people are walking barefoot!' exclaimed Veer.

'Yes, Veer. Sai Baba used to walk barefoot. He seldom wore shoes. It is very difficult to walk all the way and walking barefoot, even more so. People get blisters on their feet, in addition to muscle aches and cramps, but they still soldier on,' said Amma.

'Like the people we saw in Tirupati, who were climbing the stairs on their hands and knees!' said Veer.

'That's right, Veer. They were going to see Venkateswara,' said Amma, ruffling his hair.

'Why are they walking all the way, Amma?' asked Shiv. 'Why don't they just drive?'

'Well, they can. But they choose to walk the entire distance. They love Baba and it is their way of showing their devotion for him. People believe that Baba will take care of them and make their wishes come true. They surrender all their worries and their problems to him and it makes them stronger. Devotion and belief are very powerful.'

'I don't understand,' said Shiv.

'Let me ask you a question,' said Amma. 'When you go on the field to play a cricket match, do you feel nervous?'

'Yes, a bit. I always get butterflies in my tummy!' said Shiv.

'What if you said a little prayer to the Universe, saying I turn over all my worries to you. And if that allowed you to focus on the game and not get anxious, wouldn't that be great?'

Shiv was quiet, listening intently.

'That's what it's like when you surrender to a power higher than you. It takes away all your stress and gives you the strength and energy to focus on your work,' said Amma.

'Let me tell you about Sai Baba,' Amma continued. 'To start with, Sai Baba was not his real name.'

'Really?' asked Shiv looking puzzled, 'What was his name then?'

'No one knows his birth name,' said Amma, 'Baba never revealed much to anyone about his past. We don't know where he was born, who his parents were, or what religion he was born into.'

'How did he get the name Sai Baba then?' asked Shiv, looking even more perplexed.

'For that, you will have to listen to a story,' said Amma. 'And that story begins around the year 1854, when a handsome young man arrived in the village of Shirdi. Now how many years ago is that, Veer?' she asked.

'I knew you would ask that, Amma. I'm not doing any silly maths! This is a holiday,' replied Veer.

'165 years!' chimed Shiv.

'Is your name Veer?' said Amma, giving Shiv a glare.

She continued, 'The villagers first saw the fellow seated under a huge neem tree, deep in meditation. They were surprised to see someone so young meditating with such concentration for days and nights, oblivious to the heat and the cold. The young man kept to himself and was a mystery. They thought he was mad as he would often speak to himself, or laugh out loudly and sometimes even curse in anger. The children in the village would taunt him with cries of *pagal* and even throw stones at him and depending on his mood, the man would either indulge them or scare them with loud shouts and toss the stones right back at them.'

Shiv and Veer started giggling.

'He would wander in and out of the forest near the village. Then, after a few months, just as suddenly as he had arrived, he disappeared from Shirdi,' said Amma. 'After a few years had passed, he returned to Shirdi as part of a wedding procession.'

'Was he getting married?' asked Veer.

'No, he wasn't,' answered Amma. 'He was invited to a wedding in Shirdi as the guest of the groom's family who hailed from a neighbouring village. The marriage party was travelling in bullock carts and once they reached the outskirts of the village, they stopped at a small temple there. The carts were unharnessed and the members of the party descended one by one, as did the young man.

'The village priest, Mahalsapati, who had come out to greet the travellers was mesmerized by this young man as he saw him alighting from the cart. The man had a magnetic quality about him that attracted people and made them notice him. Mahalsapati welcomed the fellow by saying "Ya Sai" meaning "Come Saint". "Ya" means "welcome" in Marathi and "Sai" means saint in Persian. The young man was none other than Baba and that is how he came to be called Sai. The word "Baba", which means "father", was probably added later as a sign of respect.

Shirdi

'After the marriage ceremony, the procession returned to the nearby village, but the young Sai remained and stayed in Shirdi for the rest of his life,' said Amma.

'He started living under the same neem tree as before. In fact, that neem tree still stands in Shirdi,' said Amma.

'Whoa!' exclaimed Veer, 'Can we see the tree?'

'Yes indeed, we can,' said Amma.

'Wow! So many places to see, Amma,' said Shiv excitedly, 'a shrine, a mosque, a museum, and now we can add the neem tree to the list!'

'I have a question, Amma,' said Veer. 'Why did the priest call him by a Persian name?'

'The priest probably thought that Baba was a Muslim saint because of the clothes he was wearing. Baba used to wear a long white robe called *kafni* and tie a white cloth around his head, which was the way Muslim ascetics of the time used to dress,' said Amma.

'He also called himself a fakir. Muslim holy men of the time, who wandered and survived solely on alms, were called fakirs. Baba was a true fakir. The word fakir comes from the word "faqr", which means poverty. A fakir embraces poverty so that he can be free from any kind of attachment to physical objects. Baba used to say, "Poverty is my pride. Embracing poverty is better than being a king and it is better than being rich because God is always a friend of the poor."

'Fakirs are generally Sufis; hence, it was thought that Baba may have been Sufi or the disciple of a Sufi saint. Who remembers who a Sufi is?' asked Amma.

'Sufi means wool,' said Veer. 'You told us when we went to Fatehpur Sikri!'

'That's right, Veer,' said Amma. 'The wool refers to the rough woollen cloaks worn by Sufi saints.'

'Like Salim Chishti!' said Veer.

'Yes, like Salim Chishti, the famous Sufi saint,' replied Amma and smiled. 'But who are Sufi saints?'

'They are saints who meditate and pray and are disciples of Gurus,' answered Shiv.

'Yes, they are disciples of wise masters called shaikhs,' said Amma. 'They believe in love and devotion to God and that there is no greater purpose in life than to bring happiness to the human heart. They also believe that love blossoms through poetry and music and they convey their love for God by singing devotional songs and this celebration is called *sama*.'

'Like the songs we heard people singing at the dargah of Salim Chishti!' said Veer eagerly.

'Yes indeed, like the qawwalis we heard,' said Amma. 'In fact, Sai Baba loved listening to qawwalis. Baba loved to sing and dance as well. There was a place for Muslim travellers, a kind of rest house, called Takia, which was close to the neem tree under which Baba used to meditate. Baba would often spend time in the Takia at night, singing and dancing with other Sufis and devotees. He would tie small tinkling ornaments or trinkets, *ghungroos*, around his ankles and dance in ecstasy. He would sing devotional songs in Persian, Arabic and Hindi. One of his favourite poets was Kabir, and he would often sing his poems.'

'Wow! Baba knew so many languages?' asked Veer.

'Yes, Veer. He did,' said Amma.

'Who was Kabir, Amma?' asked Shiv.

'Kabir was a famous poet and saint who lived in the fifteenth century and was a big influence on Baba. He was a Muslim weaver and wrote in Avadhi and Brij, which are dialects of Hindi that people of the region spoke at the time. His poetry was about devotion and finding God within us and he challenged the need for religious rituals. One of his many well-known poems says "Jaise til mei tel hai, jyon chakmak mein aag, tera sai tujh mein hai, tu jag sake to jaag", meaning "Just as a seed contains oil, fire is present in the flint stone, the Divine is inside you, realize this if you can."

'In fact, some of Kabir's poems are a part of the Guru Granth Sahib,' continued Amma.

'The same Guru Granth Sahib we saw being carried in a palanquin in the Golden Temple!' said Veer.

'Yes,' said Amma. 'I am happy you remember!'

'It is clear that Baba viewed Kabir's life as exemplary and once said, "I was Kabir and used to spin yarn." He also said, "As a boy, I used to weave shawls, and my father was so pleased with my work that he gave me a gift of five rupees."'

'How come we never get money from you or Dada?' said Veer.

'Well if you start weaving, I may start giving you money!' said Amma.

'Yeah Veer, no one is giving you money for free, lazy bones,' said Shiv.

'Amma, why didn't Baba say who his parents were or what his religion was?' asked Veer.

'Baba never gave importance to these questions. He did not like being asked about his religion or where he came from. In fact, when people would ask him such questions, he would often become angry.'

'Why would he get angry, Amma?' asked Shiv.

'Because he could not understand why people were so keen to know which religion he was born into. Baba used to always say "Sabka malik ek", which means that there is one God. He believed that different religions were different ways of reaching the same God. So when Muslims used to come to him for guidance, he would tell them to read a relevant passage from the Quran and when Hindus used to visit him he would recommend that they read the Gita. Baba was well versed with both the Hindu and the Muslim scriptures and would often quote from both.'

'How come Baba knew so much about the Gita and the Quran, Amma?' asked Shiv.

'Again, no one knows Shiv. But it is clear that he had studied the scriptures and holy books of both religions in depth. Some devotees say that Baba told them his Guru was a person called Venkusa, a Hindu. Some say Baba said his Guru was a person by the name of Roshan Shah, a fakir.'

'Though we don't know for sure, it is believed that Baba was raised by a fakir. After a few years, the fakir passed away, and unable to cope with bringing up the boy, the fakir's wife placed him in the care of a Hindu scholar called Venkusa. Venkusa is thought to have been a devout Hindu who spent his time studying the scriptures and going for pilgrimages. No one really knows how many years Baba lived with the fakir and with his Hindu Guru, but they both must have had a strong influence on him as from a young age, Baba had discarded all thoughts of worldly pursuits and decided to lead the life of an ascetic.'

'Who is an ascetic, Amma?' asked Shiv.

'An ascetic is a person who leads a life of prayer and fasting and does not chase money or physical possessions,' explained Amma and continued. 'Baba always had God's name on his lips. His favourite sayings were "Allah Malik", meaning "Allah is the master" and "Allah Rakhega Waisa Rehna", meaning "Be happy with what one has." The names of

Krishna and Ram were equally dear to him. In fact, his favourite god was Hanuman.'

'Just like you, Amma!' said Veer excitedly. 'No wonder you like Sai Baba.'

'Yes, Veer. Isn't it special that Sai Baba loved Hanuman too?' said Amma. 'As a matter of fact, there is a Hanuman temple near the mosque that Baba lived in. And it's still there today.'

'I want to go there too!' declared Veer.

'Yes, yes, we will see everything,' suggested Amma.

'The shrine, the mosque, the museum, the neem tree . . .' said Veer.

'And the Hanuman temple!' said Shiv. 'That's five places to see now!'

'Yes, you can be our tour guide,' said Amma, smiling. 'Every day, when Baba would step out of the mosque, he would stand and look at the Hanuman temple for a long time. Sometimes, he would chant and sometimes, he would make hand gestures and draw symbols in the air.'

'What was he doing?' asked Shiv.

'No one knows for sure,' said Amma. 'He seemed to be having a private conversation with Hanuman. What we know is that Baba was very attached to Hanuman. Once, he said to a devotee, "You want to know who my parents are? There, see him, Lord Hanuman," pointed to the Hanuman temple.'

As their car ambled along the road to Shirdi, the countryside slowly gave way to bigger clusters of concrete settlements.

'We should be reaching soon,' said Amma looking out of the window. 'The Shirdi that you will see is very different from the place it was when Sai Baba arrived there. The name Shirdi comes from the Marathi words "shiladhi" or "shailadhi", which means "sugar cane", because of the large number of sugar cane fields in this area. At the time, it was a small, obscure village. Life was simple and serene.'

'Though India was under British rule, Shirdi cared little. The villagers were busy with their farming and in trying to feed their families. There was no electricity and no running water in people's homes. There was a well, a few shops and a few temples. The village was made up of about two hundred houses connected by narrow alleys and about a 1000 people lived here.'

'What! My school has more than a 1000 students!' said Shiv.

'Yes I know, but remember, I am talking about a hundred-and-fifty years ago,' said Amma. 'Today, more than 20,000 people live in Shirdi and eight to ten million people come to visit Baba's shrine every year from all over the world.'

'Wow! That's half the population of Mumbai!' said Shiv.

'Yes indeed, it is!' said Amma.

'Look, it seems everything here is named after Sai Baba,' said Veer excitedly, pointing to a hoarding that read 'Sai Baba Hotel'. Another read 'Sai Restaurant'.

Bhakti Mathur

'Looks like we've reached Shirdi!' said Amma, as the car made its way slowly into a street lined with restaurants and small shops. The shops seemed to be selling a whole range of things — statues and pictures of Sai Baba, flowers, souvenirs, snacks and a jumble of knick-knacks and trinkets.

The boys looked out of the car window at the hustle and bustle around them. Soon, the car reached the hotel where they would be staying for the duration of their visit.

'Let's get some rest now,' said Amma, getting out of the car. 'We have an early start tomorrow.'

Shiv looked at Amma suspiciously and said 'Not again, Amma! Don't tell me we are going to the temple early in the morning!'

'You always make us do this,' complained Veer. 'I am not getting up early.'

'Come on . . .' Amma started to say, but before she could finish, the boys had run inside the hotel.

Amma caught up with them but they refused to talk to her. 'What if I tell you that this hotel has something you both will love,' said Amma, trying to coax them.

'What?' said Shiv, still looking rather indignant.

'Well, follow me, I'll show you,' said Amma, as she led the way across the hotel lobby to the lawns at the back.

The boys followed her grudgingly but soon their frowns turned into big smiles.

'Veer, look! Cricket nets!' squealed Shiv.

Before Amma knew it, they had borrowed a bat and a ball from the hotel attendant and Shiv was bowling to Veer, both having forgotten what they were upset about mere minutes ago.

Tired after an hour of cricket and the long journey earlier, the boys easily fell asleep after an early dinner at the hotel. Even so, Amma struggled to get them out of bed a few hours before dawn. Promises of extra time at the cricket nets and bribes of their favourite candy finally did the trick.

It was a clear cloudless night and the moon was still high in the sky when Amma, Shiv and Veer arrived at the Sri Samadhi Mandir. The golden spire above the temple dome shone brightly in the night, reaching up as if to touch the dark sky above. The temple itself looked unassuming. Amma, Shiv and Veer stood in an open courtyard, in a long queue to enter the temple.

Shiv rubbed his eyes and Veer yawned, tugging at Amma's dupatta. The long winding line inched ahead.

'This is taking soooo long, Amma,' complained Shiv.

'Let me tell you the story behind this temple,' Amma began to try and engage the boys. 'This temple is built on land that Baba himself tended to as a gardener.'

'Baba was a gardener?' asked Shiv.

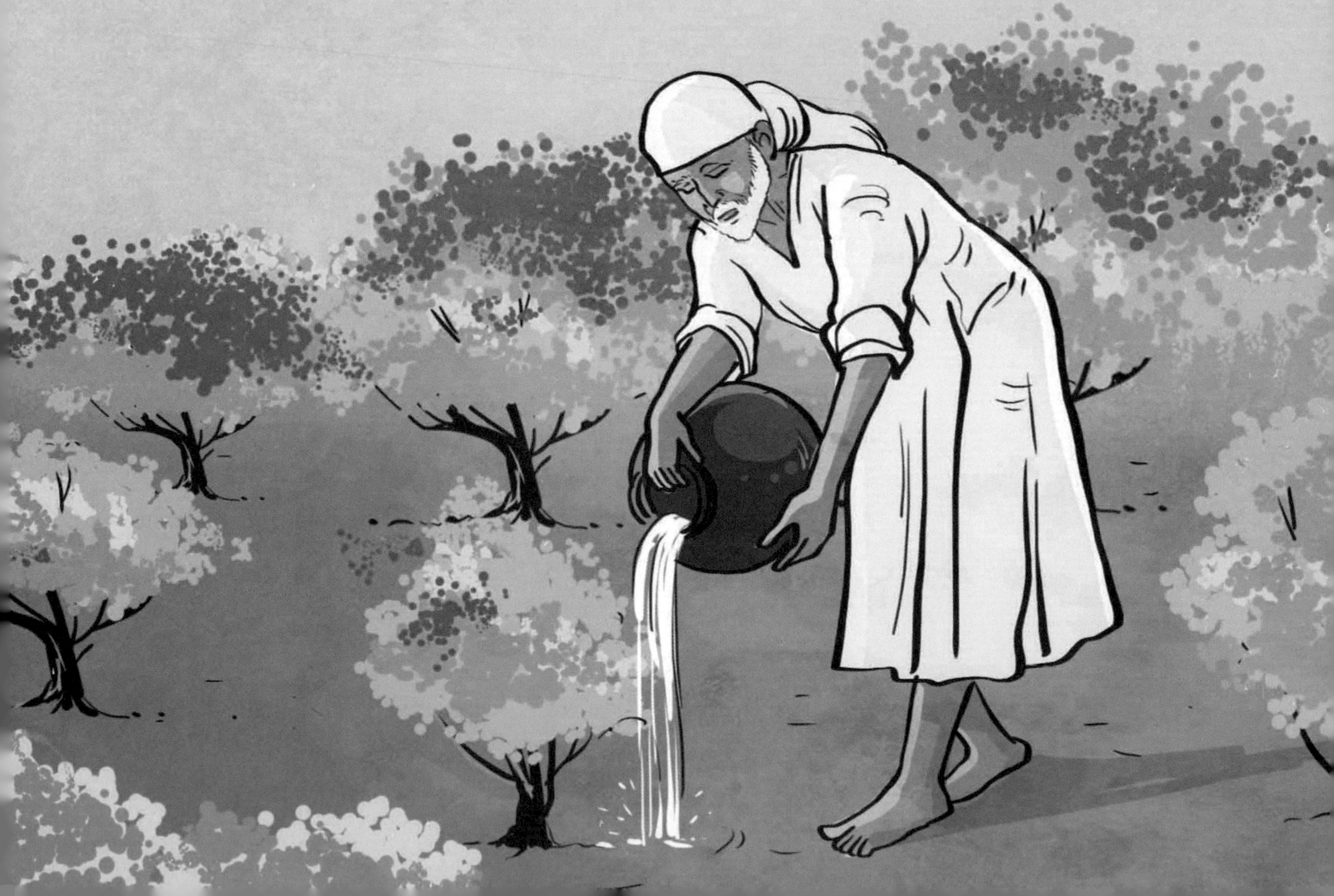

'Baba loved gardening,' said Amma. 'When he came to Shirdi, he would go to the villages nearby and bring back seedlings of marigold and jasmine. He would plant them, nurture them and even talk to them as if he was cajoling them to grow and blossom.'

Shiv and Veer started giggling at the image of Sai Baba bending over his plants and talking to them.

'In fact, Baba became famous as a healer because of his vast knowledge of medicinal plants and herbs. People started coming to Baba for a cure for some disease or the other and Baba would treat them with herbs and leaves.

'Baba began to cultivate a garden and little did he know that years later, it would be overlooking his own shrine,' said Amma. 'This temple was built three years before Baba passed away. Baba had a wealthy devotee by the name of Gopalrao Booty, who came up with the idea of building this temple in honour of Lord Krishna and as a rest house or *wada* for devotees who travelled to Shirdi to meet Baba. Baba liked the idea and the temple's construction began.

'Every day, while passing by as he begged for alms, Baba would give suggestions for the ongoing work. He told Gopalrao, "Once the temple is built, we will live in it forever with joy."

'Now Baba had a brick, which he used to always keep close to him. Sometimes he would use it as a pillow, other times he would rest his hand on it. This brick had been gifted to Baba by his Guru and was a sign of his Guru's presence and love.'

'Though we don't know who Baba's Guru was, we can be sure that Baba loved him dearly. Baba used to tell stories about how he would sit and lovingly gaze at his Guru for hours and how he would become restless in his absence. He used to say that everything he knew and everything he had become was by his Guru's grace and blessing.'

'Two months before Baba died, the brick broke. Baba was inconsolable. He said that he had lost his companion, the physical reminder of his Guru and with the breaking of the brick, his connection with the world had broken.'

Shiv and Veer were fully awake by now, captivated by the story.

'Baba did two more things that showed he knew his end was near,' said Amma.

'A few months before he died, he sent a garland of flowers with a message to his close friend Banne Miya, a renowned Sufi. The message read "Nau din, nau tarikh, allah miya apne duniya le jayega, marzi allah ki," meaning "On the ninth day and ninth night, Allah will call me to his world, it is the will of Allah." As per the Islamic calendar, this falls in the holy month of Ramzan. Banne Miya looked at the sky and tears began to roll down his cheeks.'

'Baba also sent a message, along with Rs 250, this time to Shamsuddin, who was another Sufi and an old friend of Baba's. The money was to be given to singers who sing "moulu", devotional songs and qawwalis. Hearing this, Shamsuddin also began to cry. He too realized that his old friend from Shirdi was going to leave his physical body.

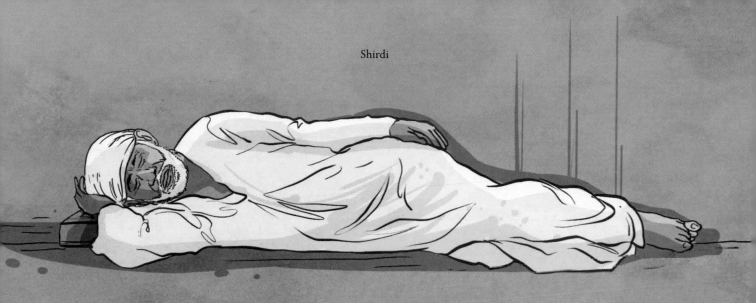

'Eight days before Baba passed away, an interesting incident occurred,' said Amma. 'A huge cart stopped in front of the mosque where Baba lived. On the cart, was a caged tiger.'

Shiv and Veer gasped.

'The tiger was clearly unwell. Its keepers used to exhibit the tiger, going from village to village to earn money. The tiger had fallen sick and its keepers had tried many remedies to cure him, but to no avail. They had brought the tiger to Baba in the hope that Baba would be able to heal him.'

The keepers told Baba about the tiger's condition. 'Bring him in here,' said Baba. 'I shall relieve him of his suffering.'

'The tiger's cage was wheeled into the mosque and Baba ordered the animal to be released. It looked fierce, even though it was unwell. The people gathered there stared at the beast in fear and amazement. The tiger slowly walked up the stairs of the mosque and sat down with its two front feet extended towards Baba. Baba's eyes glowed as though there was a fire within them. The tiger looked up at Baba, thrashed its tail on the ground three times, gave out a terrific roar and fell down dead.'

Baba asked the tiger to be buried nearby.

'The tiger is buried close by?' said Veer in a high-pitched voice. 'Can we go and see the place?'

'Yes, we can,' said Amma and carried on.

'Baba's health had been deteriorating rapidly and he breathed his last on 15 October 1918. It happened to be an important day for the Hindus, for it was Vijayadashmi, the tenth day of the festival of Dussehra as well as for the Muslims, as it was the month of Ramadan. Even in death, he seemed to be embracing both the communities. His last words were, "I am not feeling well. Carry me to the wada."

'Baba was then carried here and buried in the place where the image of Krishna was supposed to have been placed. Many years later, a huge statue of Baba was built and installed in front of his tomb.'

'Can we see the statue, Amma?' asked Shiv.

'Yes, we are lining up to see both the statue and the tomb, Shiv,' replied Amma.

'The news of Baba's passing spread quickly and thousands came to the wada to get his blessings, queuing up for many hours. Before the burial, Baba was given a final bath. Then a white cloth was spread over his body and his grieving devotees gazed at Baba's body one last time. The fakir who lived in tattered clothes all his life was given a procession fit for a king through the lanes of his beloved Shirdi,' said Amma.

'Baba's beloved brick was broken into small pieces and scattered across the open ground where his body was to be placed. His chillum, *satka*, a needle and stitching material, with which he repaired his torn kafni, were also placed inside,' Amma continued.

'Amma, what is a chillum?' asked Shiv.

'And what is a satka?' added Veer.

'One by one, you two. Let me finish what I was saying first,' said Amma and continued. 'Various layers of cloth were also set down and finally, Mahalsapati and Gopalrao, along with Baba's other devotees, lowered Baba's body into the earth.'

'To answer your question Shiv, a chillum is a hookah or a clay pipe used for smoking,' explained Amma.

'Baba smoked!' said Shiv, looking shocked.

'Many sadhus at the time smoked chillums,' said Amma. 'Baba hardly had any bad habits. We can live with this one bad habit of his, can't we?'

'A satka is a short, sturdy stick,' explained Amma. 'Baba used to shake the satka, wave it in the air or beat it on the ground whenever he wanted to scold someone or drive out something. There is a story about how when a cyclone hit Shirdi, the villagers panicked and ran to Baba for help. He simply shook his satka and ordered the storm to stop.'

'Did the storm stop?' asked Veer.

'Yes, it did!' said Amma.

'How can a stick make a storm go away?' said Shiv.

'Think of it like Harry Potter's wand,' said Amma with a smile. 'Maybe Baba cast a spell on the storm saying *Stormitis*!'

Shiv started to ask another question, but by then they had reached the entrance of the temple and were ushered into a waiting room with about two hundred other devotees. The congregation moved forward slowly and the three moved along with the crowd. Fervent cries of 'Sri Sachidananda Sadguru Maharaj ki jai' filled the air.

Veer tugged at Amma's arm and she bent down to listen. 'What is everyone saying?' he asked.

'They are saying "Salutations to Sai Baba",' explained Amma.

'Where is Sai Baba's statue?' asked Shiv, who was taking in the sights and sounds.

'You said he is buried here, Amma,' said Veer.

'Yes, his shrine and statue are both in the hall ahead,' she said, holding each of their hands tightly.

The crowd swelled forward, spilling into the main prayer hall.

'We are almost there,' said Amma softly. The three joined the hundreds of devotees who were straining to catch the first glimpse of Sai Baba's image.

And then they saw it; an exquisite statue of Sai Baba, shining like the sun. Carved out of Italian white marble, the life-like image was seated on a golden throne that stood on a rectangular pedestal also made from marble. It felt as though Baba himself was looking down upon the congregation. His face looked majestic with his mysterious half smile, his magnetic eyes gazing benignly on the hundreds of devotees who had come to seek his blessings.'

The statue was draped with orange silk that was embroidered with fine gold; a matching cloth was tied around his head. His forehead was adorned with a tilak, a huge garland of flowers rested on his neck and a gold-coloured crown sat upon his head. Rose petals were strewn on and around his feet. A gold-coloured canopy hung over the statue. The walls behind and all around were gilded in gold with intricate carvings of flowers, gods and goddesses. On the right side of the statue, the word 'Saburi' was carved in large, golden letters and on the left side was the word 'Shraddha'.

Amma, Shiv and Veer were transfixed by the vision in front of them. For a few precious moments, they were oblivious to everything except for the deep connection that they felt with the deity. It was as if they were alone in the temple with Baba.

In front of the statue was Baba's tomb. It was covered with a red silk cloth and rose petals were strewn across it. The statue and the tomb were both surrounded by a marble enclosure.

As they watched, a group of priests and musicians entered and made their way to the front of the tomb. The priests were dressed in white dhotis and kurtas and the musicians wore knee-length red kurtas with red and gold oval-shaped turbans.

A hush fell over the crowd. The priests started singing, their melodious voices filling the prayer hall, accompanied by the sounds of the tabla and the *manjira*. The soulful words of the *arti* reverberated through the temple walls, filling every ear, heart and soul. The fragrance of sandalwood from the incense sticks filled the air. The flames of the arti lamp against the backdrop of Baba's shrine and statue created a colourful kaleidoscope.

'Joduniya kar charani thevila matha, parisawi vinanti majhi sagurunatha . . .' the priests sang and the devotees joined in.

Even though Shiv and Veer did not understand the words, they were spellbound by the music, their bodies swaying gently to the tune of the song.

Even after the priests had finished singing, the notes seemed to echo all around them, and it took a minute or two for the gathering to recover, as if they were gradually being released from a hypnotic spell.

'Amma, what were they singing?' asked Shiv with wonder.

'This is called the Kakad arti or the morning arti. It's in Marathi and is sung in praise of Sai Baba. It means, "With folded hands, I lay my head at your feet. O Sadguru, please listen to my entreaty. I want to remain at your feet forever." It goes on to ask him to wake up and get to work to protect his devotees.'

'Just like the song we heard in Tirupati,' said Shiv.

'Yes, similar to the "Suprabhatam"!' answered Amma.

The three of them turned back to the statue and saw two priests climbing the marble pedestal. One of them gently removed the orange drape from Baba's statue as the other

poured milk over the statue and wiped it lovingly with a towel.

'Baba's getting a milk bath!' whispered Shiv.

'Yes, Baba gets a bath every morning,' said Amma. 'He is offered breakfast, lunch and dinner and has his clothes changed four times a day, before each arti. At night, a net is hung up, and the tomb is covered with a special white cotton cloth, the kind that Baba's kafni was made of.'

Just then, a new set of clothes was handed over to the priest and Baba was dressed in purple silk with a matching purple head cloth. The crowd slowly moved forward and one by one, people paid their respects by bending down and touching their heads to Baba's tomb.

'This is people's way of showing their love for Baba, giving thanks and praying to him. It is believed that even after saints die, they continue to send us their blessings. You can ask for Baba's blessings too,' said Amma, as she bent forward to touch her head to the tomb. Shiv and Veer followed suit.

Just then, one of the priests tapped Amma on her shoulders and placed the head cloth that Baba had been wearing in her hands saying, 'This is for you.'

Amma was taken aback and took the cloth with folded hands, a smile on her face.

'Amma, how come the priest gave the cloth to you?' asked Shiv.

'I don't know, Shiv,' said Amma. 'I think Baba is blessing me,' she said in a voice choked with emotion.

Taking once last look at the statue of Baba, Amma stepped out of the prayer hall. Shiv and Veer followed her and once they were outside the main shrine, a fight erupted between the two, both claiming Baba's headgear.

'Amma, can I have it?' asked Shiv.

'But Amma, I want it too,' argued Veer.

'No Amma, he is so careless. He will lose it,' retorted Shiv.

'Stop fighting this instant! I am not giving it to either one of you. This will be kept in the mandir at home, next to Hanumanji's *murti*,' said Amma firmly.

'Amma . . .' groaned Shiv.

'Baba loved Hanuman, so that's the right place for this cloth. And Shiv, let me tell you what Baba told a man who used to say bad things about his brother,' said Amma.

'What?' asked Shiv.

'A devotee of Baba used to constantly criticize his own brother in front of everyone.

"He's so mean, he's so lazy, he's a miser," he would go on endlessly. One day, Baba took the devotee to where a pig was rummaging through garbage and said, "Look at the joy with which this pig is eating dirt and dung. You are no different than him, bad-mouthing your own family.'"

'Now you can't say anything bad about me, Shiv, because Baba will turn you into a pig!' said Veer with a big smile.

Amma and Shiv started laughing.

'Do you remember the two words on the wall, written on either side of Baba's statue?' asked Amma.

'Oh yeah!' exclaimed Shiv, remembering. 'What do they mean?'

'The words are Shraddha and Saburi,' said Amma. 'That was Baba's philosophy of life. Shraddha means faith. It means knowing that no matter how difficult a situation may be, you have the strength to go through it with calmness, courage and grace. The problem may or may not be solved, but faith itself is the miracle that will help you through tough times.'

'Saburi means patience,' continued Amma. 'It does not mean waiting for something to happen. It means working with the belief that you will get what you desire when the time is right.'

Shiv and Veer were quiet.

Shirdi

'There's the museum,' pointed Amma to a small double-storeyed building across the courtyard from the temple. The boys followed Amma into the building and up a staircase, where Baba's belongings were on display in glass cases along the walls.

'Look, it's Baba's clothes!' exclaimed Veer, pointing to the white-coloured kafni.

'That must be his chillum!' said Shiv.

'And there's the satka!' said Veer.

'Amma, what are these?' asked Veer, pointing to a few big cooking pots.

'These are the pots that Baba sometimes used for cooking. He used to cook for his devotees,' explained Amma. 'He would shop for all the ingredients, haggle with the shopkeepers, though end up paying them far more than what they had negotiated. He would wash and cut the vegetables, place them in these pots called handis and cook the food himself. When the huge pot came to a boil, Baba would roll up his sleeve and put his hand in the broth and stir it with his bare hand. Wouldn't it have been wonderful eating food cooked by Baba?' said Amma.

'Come, it's time to see the place where Baba spent his time when he first came to Shirdi,' continued Amma.

'The neem tree!' said Veer, following Amma as she led the way.

Soon, they arrived at a huge tree standing proudly with its branches spread across the spring sky, its leaves sparkling with the morning dew.

'This is the tree that gave shelter to Baba when he first arrived here,' said Amma, visibly moved. The tree was enclosed in a steel barricade to protect it from the crowds. Some people were doing pradakshina or circumambulating the tree, others were sitting quietly, and some were burning incense in front of a statue of Baba that stood in front of the tree in a small marble shrine.

Amma, Shiv and Veer walked around the tree.

'This place is known as "Gurusthan", which means "the place of the Guru",' said Amma. 'This place was very special to Baba and he loved burning incense sticks called agarbattis here. He once said that his own Guru is buried under the tree.'

'You mean right here?' asked Shiv, wide eyed.

'Yes,' replied Amma. 'Once, some villagers were digging the ground behind the neem tree to lay the foundations of a guest house, when they came across some bricks in the soil that looked like the opening of a tunnel. Uncertain whether to proceed or not, they asked Baba what to do. He told them that under the tree lay the tomb of his Guru and requested them to leave this place alone.'

'When are we going to the mosque where Baba lived?' asked Shiv.

'That's where we are headed next,' said Amma. 'But let's sit here for a while, near this tree,' said Amma.

'I want to go to the mosque now!' said Shiv, who was getting impatient.

'Be patient, Shiv,' said Amma. 'Let me tell you how Baba came to live in the mosque.'

The prospect of a story seemed to appease Shiv and both the boys quickly huddled next to Amma and she began to narrate the tale.

'One day, Baba wandered to the temple on the outskirts of the village. Noticing how quiet and peaceful it was, he said to Mahalsapati, the priest, "What a nice place this is, for a fakir like me to live in!" But Mahalsapati refused to let Baba stay at the temple.'

'How mean,' said Veer, frowning.

'But it was hard for Mahalsapati to agree to the request,' continued Amma. 'Every time he met Baba, he was certain that this was no ordinary fakir. But he was a traditional Hindu priest. How could he allow a fakir to stay in the temple? He was worried what the people in the village would say. Not wanting to take such a risk, he had to turn down Baba's request.'

'So, Baba made his way back to the neem tree. A few months passed and a lady by the name of Bayaja Bai saw Baba. She was sure that Baba was a

44

divine soul and developed a deep affinity for him. She took it upon herself to take care of Baba and feed him. Baba spent most of his time under the neem tree, but he would often wander off across the fields and forest around the village. Every day, Bayaja Bai would cook food for Baba, pack it and then go in search of him. Sometimes, she would find him easily and sometimes, it would take her a while. But she would not eat a morsel of food nor drink water until Baba had been fed.'

'But why did Bayaja Bai want to feed Baba?' asked Shiv.

'Her philosophy was simple: to feed the poor fakir, a man of God, was as spiritual as sitting in prayer,' explained Amma.

'When she found Baba, she would lay out a banana leaf and lovingly serve him the food,' continued Amma. 'Or if he was meditating, she would make small morsels of food and slowly feed him; often, Baba would remain in meditation, but she would make sure he had eaten and only then would she leave.'

'Just like you make balls of rice and feed me sometimes!' said Veer.

Amma smiled at him and continued. 'Bayaja Bai had a young son named Tatya Kote Patil and he would frequently accompany his mother. Tatya would climb on to Baba's shoulder and Baba would chuckle and smile and indulge him. Baba loved children, you see?'

'He once said that his and Bayaja Bai's relationship went back to many lifetimes and that she was his sister in a previous birth,' said Amma.

'Is that true, Amma?' asked Shiv, looking baffled.

'I don't know, Shiv,' said Amma. 'What I can say with certainty is that Bayaja Bai looked after Baba like her own son or brother.

'Mahalsapati had two friends, Kashinath Shimpi, who was the village tailor and another named Joge, and these three men began to spend more and more time with Baba and offer him food, tobacco for his chillum and a cloth that Baba used for sitting and sleeping on, under the tree.

'One day, Shirdi was hit by a huge storm. The wind howled, the sound of thunder reverberated across the sky and rain came pouring down. Mahalsapati and his two friends ran around the whole village trying to find Baba. Bayaja Bai was very worried too. It was raining so heavily that after a while, they had to abandon the search and find shelter.'

'What happened then? Did they find Baba?' asked Veer, unable to contain himself.

'Yes, they did. When the rain finally stopped, they found Baba under the neem tree, half sitting, half reclining, in a state of deep meditation. He was drenched from head to toe and covered in mud and leaves swept up by the storm, but oblivious to it all,' said Amma.

'Everyone was amazed that Baba had survived the terrible storm. Bayaja Bai cried with joy and Mahalsapati bowed down to Baba and told him that he was no longer a guest in the village but one of them. He asked Baba if he would consider making an abandoned mosque in the middle of the village his home. Baba nodded his head and they walked towards the mosque, a small broken-down building made out of mud and cow dung. Baba looked at the dilapidated structure and smiled. "My mother has at last opened her arms to me. This is no longer a masjid. This is Masjid Ayi, my mother," said Baba. Many years later, the mosque came to be known as Dwarka Mai.'

'What does that mean?' asked Shiv.

'There is a story behind that too,' said Amma. 'Once, a devotee told Baba that he wished to make a pilgrimage to Dwarka, a city that is holy to Hindus as Lord Krishna is believed to have lived there. "There is no need for you to travel to Dwarka, this masjid itself is Dwarka," Baba replied. From that day on the mosque came to be known as Dwarka Mai.'

'Let's go to Dwarka Mai now,' said Amma, getting up and making her way out of the temple courtyard with the boys.

A two-minute walk later, the three reached the mosque, a nondescript single-storey structure with a corrugated iron roof and rough stone walls. They entered the mosque and were struck at once by the powerful atmosphere of devotion that pervaded all of Dwarka Mai. A few devotees were kneeling before a large picture of Baba, some were praying before what seemed like a small fire burning in a cage and a few were sitting in the middle of the room, reading their prayer books.

'Dwarka Mai is the real treasure of Shirdi,' whispered Amma. 'When Baba moved into the mosque, it was smaller than this. There were knee-deep holes and pits in the ground. Part of the roof had collapsed, and it looked like the other half would fall at any given moment. Yet, Baba made it his home.'

Shiv and Veer were silent, their curious gaze taking in the surroundings.

'Why is there a fire burning here?' asked Shiv, walking towards the cage.

'This is the *dhuni*,' explained Amma. 'Once Baba moved into the mosque, he built a fire using wood and oil. He would call it "Dhuni Mai" and it has been kept alight ever since Baba first lit it.'

'Whoa! For so many years?' asked Veer, looking amazed.

'Yes!' replied Amma.

'Why did he burn a fire?' asked Veer.

'Fire is considered sacred in both Hindu and Sufi traditions,' Amma elaborated. 'Fire has been used by yogis for centuries to focus their attention and meditate. Baba would wake up before dawn and sit in front of the dhuni in silent contemplation for hours.'

'He would take handfuls of *udi*, ash, from Dhuni Mai and put it in people's hands as a sign of his grace. At times, he would apply it to their foreheads. People believe that the ash from this fire has healing powers,' said Amma.

'Why did Baba give ash to people?' asked Veer.

'Ash is a reminder that one day, death will come to us all and our bodies will turn to ash. Baba used the gift of udi to remind people that chasing after material attachments was a waste of time and energy. "Nothing in this world belongs to us forever," Baba had said. "Not our houses, not money, not even our children."'

'So we don't belong to you and you can't boss us around anymore!' said Veer.

Amma laughed at his irreverence.

'Baba met with his devotees right here,' continued Amma, pointing to the space in the middle of the mosque. 'Baba's relationship with his devotees was heartfelt. He conveyed his teachings through his way of living rather than with words. He did not like giving sermons. Quite often, Baba expressed himself through stories.'

'What do you mean, Amma?' said Veer.

'Let me give you an example,' said Amma. 'One day, a very wealthy man came to meet Baba and asked him if Baba could show him the path to finding God. Baba was happy to hear this request as most people asked him to either grant them a wish or for help with a problem. Rarely did someone ask him for spiritual guidance. Baba then called a boy and, in front of the rich gentleman, requested him to go to a nearby shop and ask the shopkeeper if he would loan Baba five rupees.

'The boy left and returned shortly, saying that the shop was closed. Baba then sent him to the village grocer with the same request. The boy came back empty handed again, saying that the grocer was not at his shop at the moment. The rich man was getting impatient and repeated his question, "Baba, please tell me how to reach God. I am in a hurry."

'Baba looked at him and said, "You have more than two hundred rupees in your pocket and yet you can't offer to loan me the five rupees that I need? Till you get rid of your greed, how can you hope to find God?"

'See how cleverly Baba got his message across,' said Amma.

Across the dhuni was a large portrait of Baba placed on a throne-like platform. In the picture, Baba was seated on the floor, wearing a tattered, white kafni, with his arm leaning on a wooden balustrade. A pair of silver *padukas* was placed in front of the picture.

'Baba used to sit at this very spot where the picture is, in the same posture,' said Amma. 'The padukas are placed here, to mark the spot.'

'Where did Baba sleep?' asked Shiv.

'Baba slept right here in the mosque,' said Amma. 'Bayaja Bai's son, Tatya, and Mahalsapati used to sleep here too,' said Amma.

'Like a sleepover!' said Veer. 'What fun!'

'Yes, you could say that, Veer! And guess what! Baba used to play pranks during these sleepovers,' said Amma, with a grin.

'What?' asked Veer, his eyes lighting up.

'How?' asked Shiv, unable to hide his curiosity.

'Sometimes, after Tatya had fallen asleep, Baba would hide his belongings. The next morning, when Tatya woke up, he would be distressed to find his things missing. Baba would then pretend to help Tatya find his things. At other times, early in the morning, Baba would gently lift a sleeping Tatya, with Mahalsapati's help, and place him outside the mosque on the narrow street. Then the two would wait like children for Tatya to wake up in a state of shock, wondering how on earth he had managed to reach the middle of the lane in his sleep!' said Amma.

Shiv and Veer started laughing. 'Baba was so naughty!' said Shiv.

'Yes, just like the two of you!' said Amma, fondly.

'Let me tell you a funny story about Baba's kafni,' she went on.

'To get Baba to discard his torn kafni was a task. Time and again, people would ask Baba to get a new robe. But he would smile and say no. So when his kafni got really old, Tatya would come close to him and, pretending to ask Baba something, he would put his finger in a torn patch of the kafni and tug at it, making the tear wider. He would then point at the huge hole and tell Baba that his kafni was too torn to be worn. Baba would rant and rave and finally smile and relent.'

Shiv and Veer started chuckling.

'Dwarka Mai was full of life. Baba smoked his chillum and passed the pipe around. Everyone would take a puff and share the pleasure,' Amma carried on with the story.

'There was great intimacy between Sai Baba and his devotees and friends. Mahalsapati, Bayaja Bai, Tatya, Shyama, and others would sit around him and listen to his stories. Villagers could hear laughter coming from the mosque.'

'So it wasn't just sleepovers! Baba had play dates with his friends, too!" exclaimed Veer.

Amma and Shiv laughed.

'Baba loved his routine and even when he became famous and people started visiting him in hordes, his routine never changed. After sitting in front of Dhuni Mai, Baba washed his hands and face. Like most fakirs, Baba didn't have a bath every day. He had a bath once a week. Sometimes, Baba allowed some of his devotees to massage his legs. Once in a while, a barber came to shave his head and trim his beard.'

'What! Then I am also going to have a bath once a week!' Veer exclaimed.

'And would you like your legs massaged as well, your highness?' asked Amma, laughing.

She walked towards one corner of the mosque. A water pot stood on a stand and below that was an open mud vessel. 'This is called *kolamba*,' Amma said, pointing to the earthen bowl.

'What is it for, Amma?' asked Veer.

'Baba used to go to five houses to beg for food,' said Amma. 'And it would be the same five houses and in the same order. He would carry a *jholi*, a cloth bag, on his shoulders. All the dry food, rice, baked bread or roti and sweetmeats were placed into this bag. He also carried a tin pot, and all liquid — be it curd, dal or buttermilk — went into the pot. Baba would bless his donors by saying "Abaad-e-abaad, Allah bhala karega", meaning "May you prosper with Allah's grace".'

'When he got back to the mosque, he would make an offering of roti and some boiled rice to Dhuni Mai, which he later ate. He then mixed the rest of the food in this very pot and left it outside the mosque for the poor and stray cats and dogs.'

'This is that same pot!' said Shiv in awe.

Amma smiled and nodded.

'Baba was fond of all animals and particularly of dogs. There is an interesting story about how one of Baba's devotees, a lady called Mrs Tarkhad, took pity on a hungry stray dog who was yelping near her doorstep one day and fed it a piece of bread. Later that afternoon, when she went to visit Baba at the mosque, he looked at her, took a big burp and said, "Mother, I am still full and belching with the bread you fed me for breakfast."

'Mrs. Tarkhad was shocked and said, "But Baba, this is the first time I am seeing you today, how could I have fed you?"

'"The dog that you fed this morning is one with me. I am one with the cats, pigs, crows and all of creation. The one who sees God in all his creation is my beloved."'

'I like Baba more and more,' said Veer, 'because he likes dogs like I do. He would have loved our Frodo!'

'Yes indeed, he would have,' said Amma.

'But how did Baba know that Mrs Tarkhad had fed a dog that morning?' asked Shiv.

'I don't know,' said Amma. 'Maybe he saw her feeding the dog. But what is important is Baba's beautiful message that God lives in every living creature, human and animal alike.'

Amma walked towards one of the walls of the mosque on which there was an alcove with a set of lamps placed in front of it.

'The lamps that you see here were first lit by Baba himself. Baba loved light and the mosque was lit up with diyas the whole night. The diyas that Baba lit have never been extinguished.'

'That's impossible!' said Shiv, stunned.

'It's true,' Amma answered. 'Baba went to the local shopkeepers and begged them for oil to light the lamps and they often ridiculed him. Depending upon his mood, Baba either smiled, ignored or used to swear at them.'

Shiv and Veer started giggling.

'Baba used bad words? I like him too!' said Shiv.

Amma smiled.

'One evening, when Baba came along to ask them for oil, the shopkeepers refused to give it to him for free. Baba was disappointed but, he didn't give up. He went back to Dwarka Mai and took a tin pot, which had a little oil, added water to it and filled the lamps with the mixture. To everyone's surprise, the lamps burnt all night long.'

'But how did the lamps burn with water?' asked Shiv, looking confused.

'People believe it was a miracle or maybe Baba waved his magic wand again and weaved a spell,' Amma said with a smile.

On another wall of the mosque hung a large framed picture of Baba. 'This is probably the most famous photo of Baba,' said Amma, as the three of them stood in front of the image.

The photograph featured Baba seated on a large black stone, about two feet tall, with his right leg crossed over his left thigh, and his left hand resting on the crossed foot. Wearing a white kafni, a headscarf knotted over his left shoulder, looking relaxed yet alert, and leaning forward slightly, his expression was intense, yet compassionate.

'You see the stone Baba is sitting on in the picture?' asked Amma. 'Before Baba sat on it, the stone was used by people for washing clothes. One day, Baba happened to sit on the stone and someone took his photograph. After that, people considered the stone to be holy and it was preserved forever.'

'And that stone is right here,' said Amma, pointing to a stone kept under the photograph.

'Can I sit on it?' asked Shiv, with a naughty smile.

'No!' said Amma, firmly.

'Amma, look, a picture of a tiger!' said Veer.

'This is same tiger I told you about a while back,' said Amma.

'Oh!' said Shiv.

'There's a picture of a horse too!' exclaimed Veer.

'There's a story behind all the pictures here,' said Amma. 'There was a horse dealer by the name of Kasam. Now Kasam's prize mare had not produced a foal in a long time. Kasam came to seek Baba's blessings and promised to give him the first foal his mare produced. Soon, a foal was born to the mare and as promised, it was gifted to Baba. Baba named it "Shyam Karni", meaning "Black Ears", and loved him dearly. Baba also called him "Shyam Sundar", meaning "Black Beauty". Shyam Sundar outlived Baba and he is also buried nearby in the garden that Baba had planted.'

'What's that?' asked Veer suddenly, pointing to a large stone lying in a corner, with a sack next to it.

'That is a grinding stone,' said Amma. 'It was used to grind wheat in earlier days. There is a famous story about Baba grinding wheat.'

'"So many stories! You should write a book about them!"' said Shiv.

'Maybe I will, Shiv,' said Amma with a smile.

'Now on with the story,' she continued. 'There was a cholera epidemic raging in Maharashtra and the people of Shirdi were scared that the disease would spread to their village. One morning, when a few devotees went to the mosque, they were surprised to see Baba preparing to grind a huge quantity of wheat. After arranging a gunny on the floor, he placed a hand-operated flour mill on it, rolled up the sleeves of his kafni and started grinding the wheat. People started wondering why he was doing this. In the meanwhile, some women in the crowd decided to help. They went up to Baba, and pushing him aside, grabbed the handle of the flour mill.

Shirdi

'As the women worked, they too wondered what Baba intended to do with such an enormous quantity of flour. They thought that Baba, as was his habit, would probably distribute the flour amongst the villagers. Finally, when all the wheat was ground, Baba said, "Take this flour and sprinkle it along the village boundaries."

'People set out in different directions to carry out Baba's instructions. It turned out that the perimeter of wheat flour was Baba's defence against the cholera infection spreading to Shirdi. Baba said, "It is not the grains of wheat but cholera itself that had been crushed and cast out from the village of Shirdi."'

'Did it work?' asked Veer.

'Believe it or not, Shirdi was spared from the epidemic,' said Amma.

'How can wheat keep out an infection?' asked Shiv, looking perplexed.

'I am not sure if it was the wheat that kept the cholera out or not,' replied Amma. 'But it did drive away the villagers' fear of the disease. The perimeter of flour made people focus their energies inwards and even if cholera had spread in the village, the people would have had the fortitude to face it,' said Amma.

Amma walked towards a chest that had 'Donation Box' written on it in large letters, and put some money into it.

'We want to put in some money too!' said Shiv and Veer in unison.

Amma handed them a hundred-rupee note each, and they excitedly put it into the box.

'What is this money for, Amma?' asked Shiv.

'This is for the upkeep of the temple, the mosque and the surrounding areas,' said Amma. 'Baba never asked for money. It was only in the last ten years of his life that he started asking for money from his devotees. He would not ask everyone, he would mostly ask his wealthy devotees. Baba had no desire for money and by the end of each day, he always gave away whatever he had received to the poor and got the old temples in Shirdi repaired. He kept some for buying oil for the lamps that he lit in the mosque and to buy tobacco for the chillums. Devotees themselves used to offer Baba money. In fact, Baba would get more money in donations every day than the Governor General of India!'

Shiv and Veer gasped in disbelief.

'The government authorities heard about this and sent a few tax officials to Shirdi to collect tax from Baba. The officials expected to meet a man living lavishly in a huge house. When they arrived at Shirdi, they were surprised to see Baba sitting in his torn kafni in the midst of a run-down mosque. One of the officials looked at the other and said, "How can we ask a beggar for tax?"'

'If Baba got so much money, why didn't he use it to buy new clothes or repair the mosque?' asked Shiv.

'That's a good question, Shiv,' said Amma. 'Because Baba had very few needs and he did not believe in spending money for his own comfort. Besides, he was very happy with the dilapidated yet familiar surroundings of Dwarka Mai. There is a story about how one day, it rained so heavily that everyone feared the old mosque would collapse. Water began to collect inside the mosque and all those present begged Baba to move to Chavadi, a rest house next door. But Baba refused and was only concerned about protecting his precious Dhuni Mai.'

'Is Chavadi still there?' said Veer.

'Yes, right across the street,' said Amma. 'Let me finish the story first!'

'Eventually, one of Baba's devotees, Narayan Teli, could no longer stand the thought of Baba sleeping in the mosque during the storm. So he approached Baba, apologized for what he was about to do, quickly picked Baba up and putting him across his shoulders, ran to Chavadi. As Narayan ran, Baba hurled insults at him loudly. They entered Chavadi, Baba holding on to the man's shoulders, all the while shouting and screaming. The others followed with their mouths agape, not quite believing what Narayan had just done.'

Shiv and Veer laughed at that.

'But once inside Chavadi, Baba cooled down, and patted Teli gently. Every alternate night thereafter, Baba would sleep in Chavadi. Over time, as Baba got older, the walk across from Dwarka Mai to Chavadi became a grand affair.

'Tatya would place a golden coloured shawl around Baba's shoulders and gently lift him to his feet. With the horse, Shyam Sundar, leading the way, Baba followed with Tatya on one side and Mahalsapati on the other, walking on carpets laid on the path. A crowd of people accompanied them, singing bhajans and dancing, playing the dhol, shouting Baba's name and lighting fireworks. A silver umbrella was held over Baba's head, and as people waved flags and chanted the name of god, Baba would walk from Dwarka Mai to Chavadi. Covering the distance of a few meters would sometimes take hours.'

'Though Baba did not like any kind of show or people worshipping him, he allowed this extravagant procession out of love for his devotees. What a beautiful event it must have been,' said Amma. 'Full of joy and devotion.'

'It sounds like a party. I want to join it too!' said Veer.

'Silly, this was years ago when Baba was alive!' replied Shiv.

'But you can!' said Amma. 'Every Thursday evening, there is a similar procession. A large portrait of Baba is carried by his devotees along with his satka and padukas, from the temple to Dwarka Mai to a flurry of horns, cries and shouts. The parade winds its way through the street, which is lined with cheering crowds, and enters Dwarka Mai ten minutes later'

'The picture is then placed on a silver palanquin and carried across to Chavadi with great reverence, and is greeted there as if Baba himself is entering the guest house.'

'I want to see Chavadi!' said Veer.

So the three of them crossed the road and soon, they were at the guest house.

'I can't believe it took Baba three hours to cross the road. It took us a minute!' exclaimed Veer.

Inside Chavadi lay a plain, wooden bed.

'After Baba passed away, he was given his last bath on this bed,' said Amma.

'Another picture of Baba!' said Veer, pointing to a framed photo of Baba sitting in his famous cross-legged pose.

'This is the picture that is carried during the processions on Thursdays and during festivals,' said Amma.

'Chavadi is also the place where devotees first started performing arti for Baba,' said Amma. 'Baba would be made to sit in the midst of everyone, wearing his ragged kafni, looking like a pauper, and people would lovingly perform arti. Baba resisted this as he hated rituals, but he eventually gave in at the insistence of his devotees.'

'His eyes would glow, he would make signs, he would smile, he would glance at his devotees, and people would smile, cry and be mesmerized by him. It must have been a beautiful sight. So different from the arti now, where he is dressed up like a king, in clothes that he never wore,' said Amma.

'You mean like the one we saw this morning?' asked Veer.

Shirdi

'Yes, the artis are now performed at the Samadhi Mandir. We saw the Kakad or the morning arti. There are three other artis through the day — one at noon, called the Madhyam, another in the evening, called Dhoop and then at night, called Shej.

'I don't know about you two but, I need to rest my feet for a few minutes,' said Amma, as they made their way out of Chavadi. 'Shall we have something to drink?' she asked as she pointed to a small stall across the street serving tea and juice.

They sat down on small plastic stools and Amma ordered a cup of hot masala chai and the boys asked for orange juice.

'Amma, I have another question,' said Shiv, in between sips of his juice. 'You said almost ten million people visit Shirdi every year. How did Baba become so famous?'

'That's an interesting question, Shiv,' said Amma. 'Sai Baba has tens of millions of devotees all over India and other parts of the world who love and revere him. Many

believe he is an incarnation of God with the power to make their wishes come true. But Baba never sought this fame for himself. He was happy with the simple life of a fakir, his few daily routines and helping the people of Shirdi and a few nearby villages, who came to him seeking advice or solutions to their problems.'

'His fame spread slowly through word of mouth. His devotees would travel to other villages and towns and talk about the wonderful saint of Shirdi. They would relate stories about his miraculous deeds, his powerful healing abilities, his wisdom and knowledge. Over time, more and more people started to visit Shirdi to meet with Baba. He would evoke powerful feelings of devotion in all who spent time with him and he started being called the "Satguru" or the true Guru. Books were written about him and his fame spread to Mumbai and then across India.

'The simple life that Baba had led and the sleepy little village he lived in changed completely in the last fifteen years of his life. Shirdi became a perpetual carnival as tens of thousands of people started visiting Baba every year. The number of visitors every year kept rising even after his death and today, is in millions as you can see for yourself.

'Today, it's hard to imagine Baba as the fakir in tattered robes who walked these streets with a begging bowl, after you have seen him seated on a throne of marble, his image covered in silk, being bathed with milk and fed lavishly. But I believe it is important we remember Baba in the image of how he lived.

'You wanted to know Baba's religion?' asked Amma, looking at Shiv and Veer.

The boys nodded in anticipation, as though a secret was being revealed. 'I believe Baba's religion was love. He believed that our own hearts held the key to reaching God and our own homes were our temples and our mosques. It was nothing more complicated than that,' said Amma.

Shiv and Veer were quiet for a while.

'There is one place left on our list to see,' said Amma.

'I know!' said Veer. 'The Hanuman temple!'

'Yes!' said Amma, leaning forward to plant a kiss on Veer's cheek.

'I can see the temple standing from here, just like Baba did every day,' said Amma, pointing to the top of the Hanuman mandir.

'Let's go,' she said, holding Shiv and Veer's hands, turning back to take one last look at Dwarka Mai and Chavadi.

~GLOSSARY~

Ayi: Mother

Dargah: A shrine built over the grave of a revered religious figure, often a Sufi saint or dervish.

Hanuman: A loyal devotee of Rama and one of the key figures in the epic Ramayana. He is the son of Anjana, a celestial nymph, and Kesari, King of the Vaanara tribe.

Krishna: The ninth avatar of Vishnu and a central character in the epic Mahabharata. Also the narrator of the Bhagvad Gita (The Song of God), one of Hinduism's most popular scriptures, based on the dialogue between Krishna and Arjuna on the battlefield of Kurukshetra.

Manjira: A musical instrument, a pair of clash cymbals, which make high-pitched percussion sounds. Used as an accompaniment for devotional songs or bhajans.

Masjid: Mosque

Murti: Statue

Paduka: Footwear generally worn by mendicants and saints. Also refers to the footprints of deities and saints that are venerated.

Palanquin: A covered litter for one passenger, consisting of a large box carried on two horizontal poles by four or six bearers.

Qawwali: A form of Sufi devotional music originating from South Asia, dating back to more than 700 years. Originally performed at Sufi shrines or dargahs, it gained mainstream popularity and an international audience in the late twentieth century.

Ramadan: Also known as Ramzan, it is the ninth month of the Islamic calendar and is observed by Muslims worldwide as a month of fasting, prayer and reflection to commemorate the first revelation of the Quran to Muhammad.

Samadhi: A state of intense concentration achieved through meditation. In yoga, this is regarded as the final stage, at which union with the divine is reached (before or at death). Also refers to a shrine, tomb or monument built for a deceased saint or guru.

Tabla: A percussion instrument originating from the Indian subcontinent, consisting of a pair of drums, used in traditional, classical, popular and folk music.

Tilak: The Hindu ritual of marking someone's forehead with a fragrant paste, such as of sandalwood or vermilion, as a welcome and expression of honour when they arrive.

Vijayadashmi: A major Hindu festival that marks the end of Durga Puja, remembering goddess Durga's victory over the buffalo demon Mahishasura. The festival is also known as Dussehra, which celebrates the victory of Rama over Ravana.

Western Ghats: A mountain range parallel to the western coast of the Indian peninsula, traversing the states of Kerala, Tamil Nadu, Karnataka, Goa, Maharashtra and Gujarat.

DEVOTEES OF SAI BABA

There were many noteworthy devotees who were close to Sai Baba, besides Bayaja Bai, Tatya Kote Patil and Mahalsapati. Some of them are listed here:

Abdul Baba

Raised by a fakir and sent to Shirdi when he was 20 years old to take care of Sai Baba, Abdul Baba would clean the mosque, sweep the streets outside and wash Baba's clothes. He used to sit and read passages from the Quran in the mosque. Baba would explain the meaning of the passages, which Abdul would write down in a notebook. After Baba passed away, Abdul took care of Baba's tomb and decorated it with flowers. To this day, Abdul Baba's family members continue the tradition of offering flowers to Baba's tomb every morning. He lived in a cottage, which still stands today (close to Dwarka Mai). He is buried in the Sri Samadhi Mandir complex.

Bhagoji Shinde

A leper and one of Baba's closest devotees, he was the first person to enter the mosque every morning. He'd prepare a chillum for Baba, which they would share. Once, when Baba burnt his hand, Bhagoji massaged the burn with ghee, then placed a leaf over it and bandaged it tightly. Even after the wound healed, for years to come, Bhagoji would go through the same process every morning and Baba would allow him to do it simply because of his love for Bhagoji.

Gopalrao Booty

A multimillionaire from Nagpur, Booty became a devotee of Baba and started living in Shirdi from 1910. The Samadhi Mandir, which was initially known as 'Booty Wada', was commissioned by him.

Nanasaheb Chandorkar

A deputy collector by profession, he was a prominent devotee of Baba and used to remain by Baba's side.

Ganpatrao Dattatreya, alias Das Ganu

Originally in the police force, he was introduced to Baba through Nanasaheb Chandorkar. Das Ganu spread Baba's name across Maharashtra through his ballads and discourses. He wrote a biography on the life of Sai Baba, called *Sri Sai Gurucharitra*.

Madhavrao Deshpande, alias Shama

Shama worked as a teacher in the school adjacent to Dwarka Mai, the masjid in which Baba used to reside. He was very close to Baba and all the devotees who wanted to meet Baba used to approach him first.

Hari Sitaram Dixit, alias Kakasaheb Dixit

A well-known solicitor from Mumbai, he was largely responsible for the establishment of the Sai Sansthan and its progress after Baba's death. He managed the affairs of the Shirdi Sansthan till his own death in 1926. He maintained a diary on life in Shirdi, which covers the period 1909 to 1926. It is the first written document that contains details about Baba's life.

Annasaheb Dabholkar, alias Hemadpant

He is popularly known as the author of the work *Shri Sai Satcharitra*, which gives a detailed insight into the life and philosophy of Sai Baba. He lived in Mumbai and was a magistrate with the Mumbai government. Sai Baba named him Hemadpant after a well-known poet of the thirteenth century.

A TIMELINE OF SAI BABA'S LIFE

◆**1838** ◆ Approximate year of birth

◆**1842–1854** ◆ Sai Baba is believed to have spent twelve years with his Guru. No one knows for sure who his Guru was. It is believed that he had two gurus — a Sufi fakir and a Hindu scholar.

◆ **1854–1857**◆ Sai Baba is first seen in Shirdi, sitting in meditation under a neem tree.

◆ **1857** ◆ Disappears from Shirdi — it is believed that he lived in a mountain cave, practicing meditation, and wandered around in nearby forests meeting and spending time with other hermits and holy men.

◆ **1858** ◆ Reappears in Shirdi as a part of a marriage party and lives in the village till his death.

◆ **1885** ◆ Visit of the great Sant Anandnath Maharaj, a disciple of Shri Swami Samartha, from Yeola to Shirdi. He calls Baba a 'gem'.

◆ **1886** ◆ Baba is believed to have gone into samadhi for three days.

◆ **1889** ◆ Abdul arrives in Shirdi from Nanded.

◆ **1909** ◆ Baba begins sleeping in Chavadi on alternate nights. Devotees begin to worship Baba, resulting in the commencement of the Kakad (morning) arti and Shej (bedtime) arti.

◆ **1910** ◆ Baba's fame begins to spread beyond Shirdi, all the way to Mumbai.

◆ **1911**◆ Roofing works are carried out in Dwarka Mai, the mosque in which Baba lived, by his devotees.

◆ **1915** ◆ Construction work on Shri Samadhi Mandir begins.

◆ **1918 (October 15)** ◆ Death of Sai Baba

◆ **1954 (October 7)** ◆ Statue of Sai Baba installed in the temple on the day of Vijayadashmi.

(Source: www.sai.org.in, the official website of the Shri Saibaba Sansthan Trust, Shirdi, which is the governing and administrative body of Shri Saibaba's Samadhi Temple)

ACKNOWLEDGEMENTS

Writing this book has been quite the journey and I have been lucky in my fellow travellers who have given me unstinted support every step of the way.

My husband, Anurag, who supports me with an unstinting love and generosity that I am grateful for every day and without whom this book would have been a jumble of notes in my writing pad.

My little men, Shiv and Veer, who bring me so much joy. I hope that this book can be an answer to some of your whys, hows and whens.

My aunt, Tanuja — friend, philosopher, guide — who introduced me to Sai Baba many, many years ago and for making the trip to Shirdi so memorable.

Sohini Mitra, my fantastic editor at Penguin, for coming up with the idea for the series and convincing me to write it. I am so happy that you didn't give up on me.

The team at Penguin India — Devangana Dash, Shalini Agrawal and Piya Kapur — who worked tirelessly on this book.

To John Brennan and Rachel Ip, for being such enthusiastic readers of the drafts and for encouraging me to find my voice.

SELECTED BIBLIOGRAPHY

I am grateful to the following authors for their detailed works, which guided me in writing this book.

◆ Agarwal, Satish C. *Shirdi Sai Baba, Life Philosophy and Teachings*. Fingerprint Belief, 2017.

◆ Bharadwaja, Acharya Ekkirala, *Sai Baba The Master*. Sri Managa Bharadwaja Trust, 2015.

◆ Bharucha, Ruzbeh N. *Rabda*. Penguin Random House India 2014.

◆ Dabholkar, Govind Raghunath alias 'Hemadpant'. *Shri Sai Satcharitra.* Shri Saibaba Sansthan Trust.

◆ ——. *Shri Sai Satcharitra.* Enlightenment Press, 2016.

◆ Kamath M.V. and Kher V.B. *Sai Baba Of Shirdi – A Unique Saint.* Jaico, 1991.

◆ Rigopoulos, Antonio. *The Life And Teachings of Sai Baba Of Shirdi.* State University of New York, 1993.

◆ Shepherd, Kevin R.D. *Sai Baba of Shirdi*. Sterling Publishers, 2015.

◆ Warren, Marianne. *Unravelling The Enigma*. Sterling Publishers, 2004.

◆ Website referred to: www.sai.org.in

READ MORE IN THE SERIES

COME, EXPLORE THE PLACES WHERE WE WORSHIP!
Told through interesting stories with captivating illustrations, this new series introduces readers to the history of different faiths and their associated monuments.

Amma, Take Me to the Golden Temple

Join Amma and her children as they travel to the Golden Temple in Amritsar, the holiest seat of Sikhism. Take a tour through Harmandir Sahib. Hear inspiring stories about the Sikh gurus. Discover the heritage of Darshani Deori and the Akal Takht. Enjoy the langar offered by the world's biggest kitchen and the sacred waters at Har ki Pauri. Learn Guru Nanak's eternal message of equality, love and service.

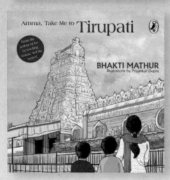

Amma, Take Me to Tirupati

Follow Amma and the boys to the world-famous temple of Tirupati Balaji. Listen to the captivating lore about a snake that became a hill range and how Vishnu came to reside on the very same hillock, first as a boar and then as a heartbroken husband. Wake up to the hymns of Suprabhatam. Savour the delicious Tirupati laddu. Enjoy the lake Swami Pushkarini. Witness the adoration of Venkateshwara's devotees.

Amma, Take Me to the Dargah of Salim Chishti

Travel with Amma and her boys to the fortress city of Fatehpur Sikri. Hear the story of why the great Mughal emperor Akbar visited the Sufi saint Shaikh Salim Chishti and had a mausoleum built in his honour. Behold the dargah of Salim Chishti, shining like a white pearl in an oasis of red sandstone, as you hear the soulful notes of azan wafting from the Jama Masjid.